In loving memory of
J.K. Ahlquist

CATegories

The Cat With The Clock Face

I've been a cat all my life. I think I was born that way. Life began for me on June 25th, 2007, in Tampa, Florida. They tell me that my mother, who lived on a ranch, left for a year long journey to explore the Everglades. Several months into her adventure, she met my father, a traveling salescat. Mom arrived back at the ranch, preggers and without dad. You know the story… single and expecting a litter. Luckily, she had a place to stay and have her babies, seven in all.

The day I was born, laughter rang out around me. "Look at the face on the black and white one! It's a face that could stop a clock!" My eyes weren't open yet, so I couldn't see what they were talking about. Was I ugly and malformed? Was I unlovable? Talk about starting out with a complex! Then I heard someone say, "It's three o'clock! Yes, three o'clock on the nose!" That must have been the exact time I was born!

Eventually my eyes opened and as I played with my brothers and sisters, someone pointed at me and asked what my name was. "Three O'Clock on the Nose" came the answer. WHAT? You can't be serious. What about "Fluffy" or "Tinkerbell?" I'd even go for "Spot!"

It wasn't until I jumped up on the bathroom sink and looked in the mirror, that I realized my fate. There they were… black clock hands placed directly on my nose!

The big hand went straight up and the small hand went off to my left, right in the middle of my little white face. I was doomed… sentenced to a life of finger pointing and laughter. I tried washing them off but realized that they were made of fur just like the rest of me. I had no choice but to deal with it and be happy. Except for the clock hands, I looked like a normal cat.

My first ten weeks of ranch life were hectic. Dogs coming and going, kittens all over the place, a cow here and there. And yes, there was pointing and laughter. Then on September 15th, in the twitch of a whisker, I found myself in a cage, in the baggage compartment of this big thing that flew through the air! Later I would find out that I was on my way to Las Vegas, Nevada. What? Why!? Little did I know, I was about to meet my adoptive human parents. Come to find out, my new dad had more fur on him than I did and all of it was on his chin!

The first night in my new home was exhausting. All I remember is falling asleep in a bowl somewhere. The next morning I found myself standing on a very cold scale in the doctor's office. "YOUR KITTEN IS UNDER WEIGHT!" the doctor told my new parents in a loud voice. "Two pounds, two ounces is not enough for a 10-week old cat. Fatten her up," she instructed! Great! I love food! No finicky cat here! I'll eat anything: cat food, buttons, plants, you name it! If it's on the floor, I'll try to get it into my mouth! In fact, it wasn't long before I could scale the wall, grab hold of a planter, hoist myself up into a bed of moss and try to eat that.

Mom always caught me before I could swallow. I'll have to admit, there was plenty of cat food; the other stuff was just an experiment.

On October 25th, my fourth month birthday, we were once again at the doctor's office. On the scale I went. This time I stared at the doctor, waiting for her response. I felt bigger, but what did I know? I'm a cat! She smiled and said, "Four pounds at four months old. Perfect!!" I was now a perfect baby cat!

What follows is a succession of pictures of me, taken by my new mom. It turns out that I love the camera and she loves clicking! Enjoy!

By Three O'Clock on the Nose
(As told to my mom, Sharon Hyla Norman)

CATegory 1

Beginnings

In the beginning,
life was a blur.

This is the face that
started it all.

Baby cat
"Three O'Clock on the Nose"
sets out to explore...

Talk about standing out
in a crowd!

At last, I see myself in the
mirror for the first time!
Actually, it looks more like
"nine o'clock" if you ask me.

The expresssion "I'm all ears" must have started here. I sure hope I grow into these things!

Could someone PLEASE help me
shave off these clock hands?

Not only do I have a clock face, I have a broken heart under my chin and a saddle made of fur.

Who designed me anyway?
What could they have been thinking?

CATegory 2

Cat Napping

Of course, all of these strange markings
have NEVER interfered with napping.

That's me at 3 months old,
in "The Silver Sleeping Bowl."

I'm not really sleeping.
It's just a long… blink.

Office work is exhausting.
YOU finish the filing.

I love napping on my daddy!

Sleeping on your back is
supposed to prevent wrinkles.

CATegory 3

Friends

Here I am with my two
friends, Nuts and Slimy.
Mom titled this picture,
"The cat with no eyes!"

I'm such a ham. These rabbits have
no interest in the camera. In fact,
they don't seem to have an interest in
anything. Did you notice the way I've
draped the end of my tail over the top of
the hutch to balance my one paw?

They say if you kiss a frog…

While visiting with my wooden cat friend, Shim Sham, we spot a bug on the ceiling.

There's nothing like getting cozy
with a Gecko…

CATegory 4

Places to Hide

That's me disguised as a fern.
Thank goodness my eyes are green!

No… everything doesn't look
green to me.

Can you find the cat in this picture?

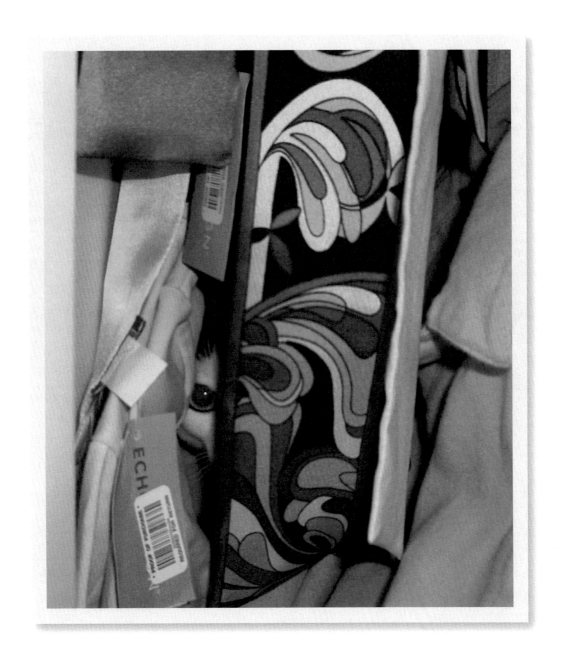

Does the red in this
bag bring out the green
in my eyes?

Here's where I hide
when I hear thunder.
I think I'm pretty well
protected here!

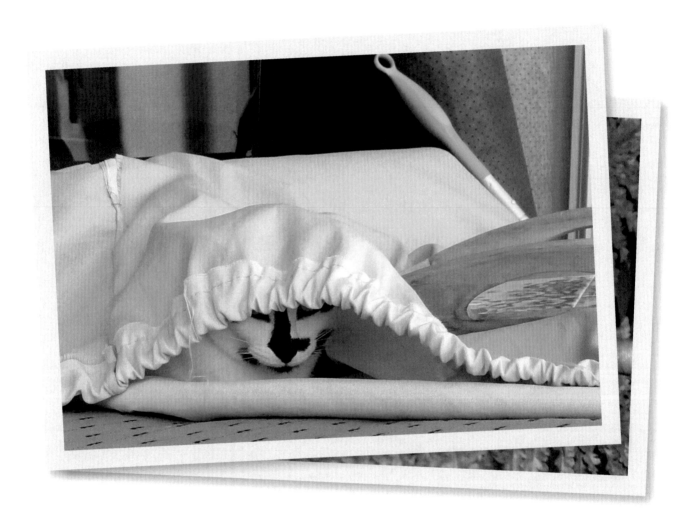

Did someone let the cat out of the bag? No, that's not right. I have to get INTO the bag first! I don't think this is going to work…

CATegory 5

Mischief

Of course I can get
out of here!

Maybe not… Mom?? Dad?? HELP!!

It's October 31st and I'm ready!
Do I scare you?

Wait a minute… this snake tastes
like RUBBER!!

And your point is...

Hey this looks tasty.

Yek! My mistake!

Hey! Look what
I found!

So THIS is what a
turkey smells like!

Boy do I feel light-headed!

SHRIMP! SHRIMP!
I want SHRIMP!

I'm so slick. They'll never
know I'm in here.

Please don't tell Dad!

Mom's plants taste good…
and are also wearable!

The green-eyed monster and
the attack of Pogo Town.

I'm NOT supposed to be on
the knick-knack shelf!

Uh, ohhhh…

I love you, Abe!

CATegory 6

Skills

"The Cat" as a center piece.
"I don't know how long I can
stay in this position!"

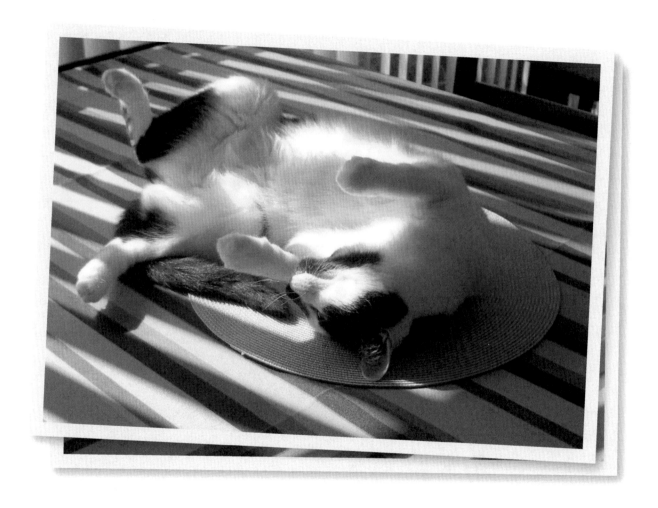

Ugh! Computer work makes my back legs tired!

Here's what
I'm looking for!
"How to order
cat toys
online!"

CATegory 7

CATchall

Are you done with your cereal?

I can't start my day without
breakfast and the newspaper.

What do you mean, I've
deleted something?
I'm just sitting here minding
my own business.

Have you ever seen a
cat with headlights?

You've gotta be kidding
me! I'll admit that I
have a great imagination,
but this is ridiculous!

There's an elephant in the room?

You're probably wondering
how I got up here!
If you own a cat, you
know the answer!

Night night! This cat modeling
is exhausting! Gotta catch a nap
before I start Book Two!

Dedication

I'd like to send out a thank you to my Mom, Sharon Norman and her husband, my Dad, Doug Cox, for their love and support and their acknowledgement that I dislike Salmon cat food. Over the last six years, I've come to realize that my little clock face has brought me more good attention than I would have ever imagined. They say that there is a moral in every story, even mine. Be proud of

your uniqueness. You are the only one like you on earth. Thank you, Mom and Dad, for always smiling at me and saying how much you care. You may think that I don't understand but I hear every word.

Because of you, I'm a well adjusted, fun loving, happy cat, who loves to lay on her back and look at the world upside down.

Three O'Clock on the Nose

Follow my blog on my website at: www.threeoclockonthenose.com

Made in the USA
San Bernardino, CA
29 November 2015